LUDWIG VAN BEETHOVEN

SYMPHONY No. 1

C major/C-Dur/Ut majeur
Op. 21

Edited by/Herausgegeben von
Max Unger

Ernst Eulenburg Ltd
London · Mainz · Madrid · New York · Paris · Prague · Tokyo · Toronto · Zürich

Ernst Eulenburg Ltd
48 Great Malborough Street
London W1V 2BN

CONTENTS/INHALT

Preface/Vorwort V

I. Adagio molto/Allegro con brio 1

II. Andante cantabile con moto 33

III. Menuetto/Trio. Allegro molto e vivace 50

IV. Adagio/Allegro molto e vivace 60

BEETHOVEN'S SYMPHONIC PRODUCTION: COMPOSITION, PERFORMANCE, PUBLICATION
BEETHOVENS SINFONISCHES WERK: DATEN DER ENTSTEHUNG, URAUFFÜHRUNG, VERÖFFENTLICHUNG

	Title and key/ Titel und Tonart	(Preliminary) principal dates of composition/ (Entwürfe) Haupt-Kompositionsdaten	First performance (all in Vienna)/Uraufführung (alle in Wien)	First edition/Erstausgabe	Dedication/Widmung
Hess 298	*sinfonia*, C minor/Moll (sketches/Skizzen)	? late 1780s/späte 1780er	—	—	—
—	*symphony*, C	*c.*1795–1797	—	—	—
op.21	Symphony no.1, C	1799–1800	Burgtheater, 2 April 1800	Hoffmeister, Vienna/ Wien, December 1801	Baron/Freiherr Gottfried van Swieten
op.36	Symphony no.2, D	1801–1802	Theater an der Wien, 5 April 1803	Bureau of Arts and Industry, Vienna/Kunst- und Industrie-Kontor, Wien, March/März 1804	Prince/Fürst Carl von Lichnowsky
op.55	Symphony no.3, E♭ (*Sinfonia eroica*)	1803–1804	Theater an der Wien, 7 April 1805	Bureau of Arts and Industry, Vienna/Kunst- und Industrie-Kontor, Wien, October 1806	Prince/Fürst Franz Joseph von Lobkowitz
op.60	Symphony no.4, B♭	1806	Lobkowitz Palace/Palais Lobkowitz, 7 March 1807	Bureau of Arts and Industry, Vienna/Kunst- und Industrie-Kontor, Wien, 1808	Count/Graf Franz von Oppersdorff
op.67	Symphony no.5, C minor/Moll	(1804–1805) 1807–1808	Theater an der Wien, 22 December 1808	Breitkopf & Härtel, Leipzig, March/März 1809	Prince/Fürst Lobkowitz and/und Count/Graf Andreas von Rasumovsky
op.68	Symphony no.6, F (*Sinfonia pastorale*)	(1807) 1808	Theater an der Wien, 22 December 1808	Breitkopf & Härtel, Leipzig, May 1809	Prince/Fürst Lobkowitz and/und Count/Graf Rasumovsky
op.92	Symphony no.7, A	1811–1812	Great Hall of the University/Universitäts-Aula, 8 December 1813	Steiner, Vienna/Wien November 1816	Count/Graf Moritz von Fries
op.93	Symphony no.8, F	1812	Großer Redoutensaal, 27 February 1814	Steiner, Vienna/Wien 1817	—
op.125	Symphony no.9 D minor/ Moll ("Choral")	(1812–1822) 1823–1824	Kärntnertortheater, 7 May 1824	Schott, Mainz, August 1826	King/König Friedrich Wilhelm of Prussia/von Preußen

PREFACE/VORWORT

Despite the well-known tradition in Beethoven criticism of assigning the composer's works to one of three creative periods, the nine symphonies are perhaps best divided into four groups. The First and Second were written during the time that conventionally marks the transition between the early and middle period. The next four belong to what may be described as the 'heroic phase',[1] which begins in 1803 and is marked by a prodigious output of highly original works on a grand scale. The Seventh and Eighth, which mark the end of the middle period, show a certain retreat from the bold directions taken in the first six works. The Ninth is Beethoven's only symphony of the last fifteen years of his life; and its unusual structure and unprecedented large performing forces place it in a category of its own.

In fact, Symphonies 1 and 2 look back to eighteenth-century Viennese classicism more than they foreshadow their composer's path-breaking achievements in the genre; the Second, in particular, enjoys a close kinship with Mozart's 'Prague' Symphony (K504) of 1786, a work with which it shares tonality, mood, and the shape of the slow introduction to the first movement. The *Eroica* was begun immediately after the Second, but

[1] The expression was coined by Alan Tyson (in his essay 'Beethoven's Heroic Phase', *The Musical Times*, CX (1969), pp. 139–41) in connection with the years 1803–5, which saw the composition of the *Eroica,* the oratorio *Christus am Ölberge* ('The Mount of Olives'), and the opera *Leonore*; but the period may be extended to include the major instrumental works that followed in their wake

Obwohl nunmehr traditionell Beethovens Schaffen in drei Perioden eingeteilt wird, ist es wahrscheinlich treffender, die neun Sinfonien in vier Gruppen zu untergliedern. Die erste und zweite Sinfonie entstanden zu einer Zeit, die nach allgemeiner Einschätzung den Übergang zwischen früher und mittlerer Periode darstellt. Die folgenden vier kann man einer ,,heroischen Phase"[1] zuordnen, die sich, 1803 beginnend, durch eine beachtliche Produktion von in höchstem Maße originären Werken großen Umfangs auszeichnet. Die ,,Siebte" und ,,Achte" als Abschluß der mittleren Periode lassen einen gewissen Rückzug von den kühnen Wegen erkennen, die er in den ersten sechs Werken dieser Gattung eingeschlagen hatte. Die ,,Neunte" ist Beethovens einzige Sinfonie der letzten 15 Lebensjahre; ihre außergewöhnliche Gesamtform und nie vorher dagewesene Aufführungsdauer machen sie zu einem Sonderfall.

Die Sinfonien 1 und 2 sind in der Tat eher eine Rückschau auf die Wiener Klassik des 18. Jahrhunderts, als daß sie die bahnbrechenden Errungenschaften des Komponisten in der Gattung erkennen ließen: besonders die ,,Zweite" zeigt eine enge Verwandtschaft mit Mozarts ,,Prager" Sinfonie KV 504 aus dem Jahre 1786, mit der sie Tonart, Grundstimmung und das Vorhandensein einer langsamen Einleitung zum I. Satz gemein

[1] Der Ausdruck wurde geprägt von Alan Tyson in seinem Essay ,,Beethoven's Heroic Phase", in: *The Musical Times*, CX (1969), S. 139–141, mit Bezug auf die Jahre 1803–05, während derer die ,,Eroica", das Oratorium *Christus am Ölberg* op. 85, und die Oper *Leonore* komponiert wurden. Doch kann man diese Schaffensperiode ebenso erweitern und die in den folgenden Jahren entstandenen instrumentalen Hauptwerke einbeziehen.

under profoundly different personal circumstances for its composer: it is the first work in which he came to terms with his increasing deafness by going far beyond the limits of musical convention. The next symphony Beethoven began composing, in C minor (the Fifth), took the genre a stage further by its concern for overall planning, its four contrasting movements being 'unified' by the presence – at different levels – of the parallel tonality of C major. In the *Sinfonia pastorale* (the Sixth) he solved the problem of large-scale organisation in other ways, by joining the last three movements to one another and by drawing a dynamic curve across the entire work.

Beethoven's progress as a symphonist did not pursue a single path, or a straight line, as seems to have been the case in the string quartets. The Fourth Symphony, which was composed quickly in the summer of 1806 and represents something of a return to classical principles (the orchestral forces required for it are the smallest for a Beethoven symphony), may have been released before the Fifth on account of unfavourable reactions to the *Eroica* after its first performance in 1805. It is more likely that memories of the artistic failure of the first concert featuring the Fifth and Sixth Symphonies prompted the composer to write a pair of musically lighter works, or at least cooler ones, in 1811–12; more than the Fourth Symphony, the Eighth marks a return to eighteenth-century symphonic dimensions.

hat. Die „Eroica" wurde unmittelbar nach der „Zweiten" in Angriff genommen, jedoch unter grundsätzlich veränderten persönlichen Umständen für den Komponisten: sie war sein erstes Werk, worin er sich mit seiner fortschreitenden Ertaubung arrangierte, indem er die Grenzen der musikalischen Konvention weit hinter sich ließ. Die nächste Sinfonie, die Beethoven zu komponieren begann, stand in c-Moll (die spätere „Fünfte") und war in Anbetracht der satzübergreifenden Anlage, deren vier kontrastierende Sätze durch die differenzierte Präsenz der gleichnamigen Durtonart C-Dur miteinander verklammert werden, ein großer Schritt in der Weiterentwicklung der Gattung. In der „Sechsten", der *Sinfonia pastorale*, kam Beethoven hinsichtlich der großformatigen Gliederung zu einer ganz anderen Lösung, indem er einerseits die letzten drei Sätze miteinander verband und andererseits das gesamte Werk mit einem wirksamen Gestaltungsbogen überzog.

Beethovens Fortgang als Sinfoniker läßt sich nicht als Einbahnstraße oder als gerade Linie verfolgen, wie es sich für das Streichquartettschaffen anbietet. Die vierte Sinfonie, im Sommer 1806 schnell hingeworfen, scheint zu den Ursprüngen der Klassik zurückzukehren – so ist beispielsweise die Orchesterbesetzung von allen Beethoven-Sinfonien die kleinste – und hat vermutlich aufgrund der mehr als zurückhaltenden Reaktion auf die Uraufführung der „Eroica" (1805) vor ihr den Vorzug der früheren öffentlichen Präsentation erhalten. Noch wahrscheinlicher ist die Annahme, Beethoven habe in Anbetracht des künstlerischen Mißerfolgs der Erstaufführung von fünfter und sechster Sinfonie sich dazu veranlaßt gesehen, in den Jahren 1811/12 ein Paar von musikalisch unbeschwerteren oder gar zurückhaltenderen Werken zu kom-

With the Ninth, of course, Beethoven resumed his pioneering role as a symphonist, combining a supreme command of sonata structures and orchestral technique with masterly control of the additional forces of chorus and solo voices to shape a type of composition hitherto unknown in serious concert music. This fusion of symphony and oratorio was by no means quickly realized. The intention to write a symphony in D minor was first expressed during the composition of the Eighth; the theme of the Scherzo was first sketched a few years later in 1815; the first sketchleaf entry describing a symphony with chorus dates from 1818.[2] By the time the Ninth was completed twelve years had elapsed since the previous symphonies; only the composition of a still more innovatory set of works, the late string quartets, remained to be achieved.

Towards the end of his life Beethoven expressed the desire to write one more symphony. Two of his companions from the late years, Anton Schindler and Karl Holz, claimed that large sections of a 'Tenth Symphony' had been sketched and that the work was complete in the composer's mind; but from the evidence of the surviving manuscripts, it appears that little, if any, progress was made on

[2] For a full account of the early plans for Beethoven's last symphony, see Sieghard Brandenburg, 'Die Skizzen zur Neunten Symphonie', *Zu Beethoven 2*, ed. H. Goldschmidt, Berlin 1984, pp. 88–129

ponieren; mehr noch als die „Vierte" kehrt schließlich die achte Sinfonie zu der üblichen Ausdehnung einer Sinfonie des 18. Jahrhunderts zurück.

Mit der neunten Sinfonie hatte Beethoven natürlich die Rolle als sinfonischer Vorkämpfer für sich zurückgewonnen, indem er den höchsten Anspruch an Sonatenhauptsatzform und orchestrale Mittel mit meisterhafter Beherrschung des Potentials von Chor und Solostimmen verband und so einen Kompositionstyp schuf, der bis dahin in der ernsten konzertanten Musik ohnegleichen war. Diese Verquickung von Sinfonie und Oratorium war indes von langer Hand vorbereitet. Erste Anzeichen zur Komposition einer d-Moll-Sinfonie gab es zur Zeit der Niederschrift der „Achten"; das Thema des Scherzos in seiner ursprünglichen Gestalt wurde 1815, wenige Jahre später, skizziert; das erste Skizzenblatt, das den Hinweis auf eine Sinfonie mit Chor enthält, datiert von 1818[2]. Bis zur Vollendung der „Neunten" waren seit den vorangegangenen Sinfonien zwölf Jahre verstrichen, und lediglich eine noch umwälzendere Reihe von Werken harrte ihrer Vollendung: die späten Streichquartette.

Gegen Ende seines Lebens äußerte Beethoven sein Streben nach der Komposition einer weiteren Sinfonie. Zwei seiner Wegbegleiter in den letzten Jahren, Anton Schindler und Karl Holz, stellten die Behauptung auf, daß weite Teile einer 10. Sinfonie in Skizzen existierten und daß das Werk im Kopf des Komponisten vollständig entworfen worden wäre. Jedoch erscheinen die überlieferten Skizzen vergleichsweise unbedeutend, da sie zu geringe, wenn überhaupt irgendwelche, Fortschritte zur Vollen-

[2] hinsichtlich einer vollständigen Darstellung der frühen Pläne zu Beethovens letzter Sinfonie vgl. Sieghard Brandenburg, „Die Skizzen zur Neunten Symphonie", in: *Zu Beethoven* 2, hg. v. Harry Goldschmidt, Berlin 1984, S. 88–129

a new work in the genre.[3]

From the point of view of performance and early reception, it is not the year 1803, but 1807 that marks the dividing line in Beethoven's symphonic output. The first four symphonies were originally intended more for private consumption, being written for and dedicated to their patrons and played mainly in aristocratic circles. The last five symphonies were written specifically for public concerts. The Fifth and Sixth, composed in 1807–8, were heard for the first time in December 1808; the Seventh and Eighth (also composed in rapid succession) at a series of concerts in the winter of 1813–14. For each pair of works, Beethoven composed – nearer the date of the concerts – an occasional piece that would provide a fitting end to a musically arduous programme; the Choral Fantasy in 1808, the 'Battle Symphony' *(Wellingtons Sieg)* in 1813. When the Ninth Symphony was first performed in May 1824, in a programme that included other Viennese Beethoven premières, its own finale provided the rousing conclusion to the concert.

dung eines neuen Werkes in dieser Gattung erkennen lassen[3].

Aus der Sicht von Aufführung und früher Rezeption markiert nicht das Jahr 1803, sondern 1807 die Trennlinie in Beethovens Schaffen. Die ersten vier Sinfonien waren eigentlich mehr für den privaten Gebrauch bestimmt: für ihre Förderer geschrieben, ihnen gewidmet und vornehmlich in aristokratischen Kreisen aufgeführt. Demgegenüber sollten die letzten fünf Sinfonien ausdrücklich dem breiten Publikum vorgestellt werden. Die 1807/08 komponierten 5. und 6. Sinfonie erlebten ihre Uraufführung im Dezember 1808, die in ebenfalls rascher unmittelbarer Aufeinanderfolgeniedergeschriebene siebente und achte in einer Folge von Konzerten während des Winters 1813/14. Als Ergänzung zu jedem Werkpaar komponierte Beethoven kurz vor der Aufführung ein Gelegenheitswerk, das ein musikalisch anspruchsvolles Programm zu einem quasi versöhnlichen Ende führen sollte: 1808 war es die *Chorfantasie* op. 80, 1813 die „Schlacht- und Siegessinfonie" (*Wellingtons Sieg oder die Schlacht bei Vittoria*) op. 91. Im Mai 1824, als die Neunte Sinfonie neben anderen Wiener Uraufführungen von Werken Beethovens dem Publikum vorgestellt wurde, war es ihr eigenes Finale, das den krönenden Abschluß der Veranstaltung darstellte.

SYMPHONY No. 1

Although there are no surviving sketches that can be linked to the composition of the First Symphony, Beethoven left behind a vast array of material for a C major

SINFONIE Nr. 1

Obgleich sich keine mit der Komposition der Ersten Sinfonie in Zusammenhang zu bringenden Skizzen erhalten haben, hinterließ Beethoven dennoch eine beträcht-

[3] The problems of the 'Tenth' are summarized and discussed by Robert Winter in an essay (in English) entitled 'Noch einmal: wo sind Beethovens Skizzen zur Zehnten Symphonie?', in *Beethoven-Jahrbuch*, X (1977), pp. 531–2

[3] Die Problematik der „Zehnten" ist aufgeführt und zusammengefaßt von Robert Winter in einem in englischer Sprache verfaßten und mit „Noch einmal: wo sind Beethovens Skizzen zur Zehnten Symphonie?" betitelten Aufsatz, in *Beethoven-Jahrbuch* X (1977), S. 531–552.

symphony projected in 1795 but abandoned the following year. Sketches for all four movements exist in various manuscript sources, and are in particular abundance for the slow introduction and the opening *Allegro*. The main theme of this movement bore a close relationship to that of the finale of the present work:[4]

liche Ansammlung an Material für eine C-Dur-Sinfonie, die er 1795 plante, im Folgejahr jedoch verwarf. Skizzen zu allen vier Sätzen gibt es in verschiedenen handschriftlichen Quellen, vornehmlich zur langsamen Einleitung und zum ersten *Allegro*. Das Hauptthema dieses Satzes steht in auffälliger Verbindung zu jenem aus dem Finale des vorliegenden Werks:[4]

The symphony was first performed on 2 April 1800 at the Burgtheater in Vienna, at a concert that also included the first public performance of the Septet op.20, and was an instant success. The reviewer for the *Allgemeine musikalische Zeitung* praised it for its 'considerable art, novelty and wealth of ideas'.[5] It was played at each of the concerts at which Beethoven's next three symphonies were performed for the first time.

Die Sinfonie wurde am 2. April 1800 im Wiener Burgtheater uraufgeführt. Das Programm enthielt desweiteren die erste öffentliche Aufführung des Septetts op. 20. Die „Erste" hatte auf Anhieb Erfolg. Der Berichterstatter der *Allgemeinen musikalischen Zeitung* lobte sie als ein Werk, „worin sehr viel Kunst, Neuheit und Reichtum an Ideen war"[5]. Bei jedem der Konzerte mit Uraufführungen einer der drei folgenden Sin-

[4] Gustav Nottebohm had dismissed the sketches for the projected symphony as 'offering little interest in themselves' (*Zweite Beethoveniana*, Leipzig 1887, p.228); but Joseph Kerman and Douglas Johnson have shown that they represent the most fully documented compositional process for any of Beethoven's works up to the late 1790s. See Kerman, *Ludwig van Beethoven: Autograph Miscellany from Circa 1786 to 1799 . . . (The 'Kafka Sketchbook')*, London 1970, vol. II, pp.166–74 (transcriptions) and pp.290–1 (commentary); Johnson, *Beethoven's Early Sketches in the 'Fischhof Miscellany'*, Ann Arbor 1980, vol. I, pp.461–9 (commentary) and vol. II, pp.163–76 (transcription). The sketch reproduced here was transcribed by Johnson from the manuscript A75, bundle 9 in the Gesellschaft der Musikfreunde, Vienna.

[5] Quoted in A.W. Thayer, *Thayer's Life of Beethoven*, rev. and ed. Elliot Forbes, Princeton 1964, p.255

[4] Gustav Nottebohm war über die Skizzen zur geplanten Sinfonie mit der Beurteilung „an sich nicht interessant" hinweggegangen (*Zweite Beethoveniana*, Leipzig 1887, S. 228); Joseph Kerman und Douglas Johnson haben hingegen nachgewiesen, daß sich anhand dieser Skizzen der am ausführlichsten dokumentierte Kompositionsprozeß aller Werke Beethovens bis in die späten 1790er Jahre nachvollziehen läßt. Vgl. Kerman, *Ludwig van Beethoven: Autograph Miscellany from Circa 1786 to 1799 . . . (The "Kafka Sketchbook")*, London 1970, Bd. II, S. 166–174 (Transkriptionen) und S. 290f. (Kommentar); und Johnson, *Beethoven's Early Sketches in the "Fischhof Miscellany"*, Ann Arbor 1980, Bd. I, S. 461–469 (Kommentar), und Bd. II, S. 163–176 (Transkription). Die an dieser Stelle wiedergegebene Skizze wurde von Johnson nach dem Autograph A 75, Konvolut 9 der Gesellschaft der Musikfreunde, Wien, übertragen.

[5] Zitiert nach A.W. Thayer, *Ludwig van Beethovens Leben*, deutsch bearbeitet von Hermann Deiters, neu ergänzt von Hugo Riemann, II, Leipzig [3]1922, S. 172.

Beethoven offered the symphony to the Leipzig firm Hoffmeister und Kühnel (later known as C.F. Peters), who published it in December 1801. It soon entered the repertory of orchestras throughout Germany: in Berlin, Breslau, Brunswick, Dresden, Frankfurt-am-Main, Leipzig, and Munich. A full score was published, without Beethoven's authorization, in London in 1809; Simrock of Bonn issued a score in 1822, the first to be prepared with the composer's knowledge.

The composer originally intended to dedicate his First Symphony to Archduke Maximilian Franz, who had been the Elector of Cologne while Beethoven was employed at the Court orchestra in Bonn. But the elector, who had fled the Rhineland in 1794 during the Napoleonic invasions, died in June 1801; and the dedication was instead given to Baron Gottfried van Swieten, an influential (if conservative) figure in the Viennese musical world who had made Beethoven's acquaintance as early as 1793.

William Drabkin

fonien Beethovens wurde die Sinfonie Nr. 1 vorgetragen.

Beethoven bot sie dem Leipziger Verlag Hoffmeister & Kühnel an (später als C. F. Peters bekannt), der sie im Dezember 1801 herausbrachte. Bald wurde die Sinfonie zum festen Bestandteil des Repertoires von Orchestern in ganz Deutschland: in Berlin, Breslau, Braunschweig, Dresden, Frankfurt am Main, Leipzig und München. 1809 erschien in London ohne Beethovens Zustimmung eine Partitur, Simrock in Bonn gab eine weitere 1822 heraus; sie war die erste, die mit Kenntnis des Komponisten vorbereitet wurde.

Es war von Anfang an Beethovens Absicht gewesen, seine erste Sinfonie Erzherzog Maximilian Franz zu widmen, der zu der Zeit von Beethovens Mitgliedschaft in der Bonner Hofkapelle Kurfürst von Köln war. Doch dieser, während der Invasion Napoleons 1794 aus dem Rheinland geflüchtet, verstarb im Juni 1801; und so wurde Baron Gottfried van Swieten – eine einflußreiche, wenn auch konservative Persönlichkeit in der Wiener Musikwelt – zum Widmungsträger; er hatte Beethoven schon 1793 kennengelernt.

William Drabkin
Übersetzung Norbert Henning

SYMPHONY No.1

I

Ludwig van Beethoven
(1770–1827)
Op. 21

 EE 3618 Ernst Eulenburg Ltd

Fl.
Ob.
Cl.
Fg.
Cor. (C)
Vl.
Vla.
Vc. e B.
Tr. (C)
Timp.
cresc.
ten.
10

Allegro con brio (𝅗𝅥 = 112)

30
Fl.
Ob.
Cl.
Fg.
Cor. (C)
Tr. (C)
Timp.
Vl.
Vla.
Vc. e B.

zu 2
Fl.
Ob.
zu 2
Cl.
2.
Fg.
Cor. (C)
Tr. (C)
Timp.
Vl.
Vla.
Vc. e B.

40
Fl.
sf
cresc.
Ob.
zu 2
cresc.
Cl.
zu 2
sf
cresc.
Fg.
sf
zu 2
cresc.
Cor
(C)
Tr.
(C)
Timp.
Vl.
cresc.
cresc.
Vla.
cresc.
Vc.
e B.
cresc.

Fl.
Ob.
Cl.
Fg.
Cor. (C)
Tr. (C)
Timp.
Vl.
Vla.
Vc. e B.
ff
1.

Fl.
Ob.
Cl.
Fg.
Cor. (C)
Tr. (C)
Timp.
Vl.
Vla.
Vc. e B.
50
60
1.
p
sf

Fl.
Ob.
Cl.
Fg.
Vl.
Vla.
Vc. e B
Cor. (C)
Tr. (C)
Vc. e B.
70
zu 2
p
sf
f

Fl.
Ob.
Cl.
zu 2
Fg.
Cor. (C)
Tr. (C)
Vl.
Vla.
Vc. e B.
sf
ff
pp
p
1.
80

90
zu 2
Fl.
Ob.
Cl.
Fg.
Cor. (C)
Tr. (C)
Timp.
Vl.
Vla.
Vc. e B.
cresc.
zu 2

100
Fl.
Ob.
Cl.
Fg.
Cor. (C)
Tr. (C)
zu 2
Timp.
Vl.
Vla.
Vc. e B.

1.
2.
Fl.
Ob.
Cl.
Fg.
Cor. (C)
Tr. (C)
Timp
Vl.
Vla.
Vc. e B.

110
Fl.
Ob.
Cl.
Fg.
Cor (C)
Tr. (C)
Vl.
Vla.
Vc. e B.
120
Fl.
Ob.
Cl.
Fg.
Cor. (C)
Tr. (C)
Vl.
Vla.
Vc. e B.

130
Fl.
Ob.
Cl.
Fg.
Cor. (C)
zu 2
Vl.
Vla.
Vc. e B.
cresc.

140
Fl.
Ob.
Fg.
Vl.
Vla.
Vc.
e B
f
sf
1.
p
Vc.
e B.

150
Fl.
Ob.
Fg.
Vl.
Vla.
p
Vc.
e B.
160
ff
Cor
(C)
Tr.
(C)

Fl.
Ob.
Cl.
Fg.
Cor. (C)
Tr. (C)
Vl.
Vla.
Vc. e B.
ff
sf
f
p
170
1.

180
1.
190
zu 2
Fl.
Ob.
Cl.
Fg.
Cor (C)
Tr. (C)
Timp
Vl.
Vla.
Vc. e B
cresc.

Fl.
Ob.
Cl.
Fg.
Cor (C)
Vl.
Vla.
Vc. e B.
1.
p cresc.
ff
cresc.
cresc.
Tr. (C)
Timp.
zu 2
200
sf

Fl.
Ob.
Cl.
Fg.
Cor. (C)
Tr. (C)
Timp
Vl.
Vla.
Vc. e B.
zu 2
sf
1.
p
f
210
p sf

Fl.
Ob.
Cl.
Fg.
Cor. (C)
Vl.
Vla.
Vc. e B.
zu 2
1.
220

Fl.
Ob.
Cl.
Fg.
Cor. (C)
Tr. (C)
Timp
Vl.
Vla.
Vc. e B.
zu 2
zu 2
zu 2

sf
zu 2
230
Fl.
Ob.
Cl.
Fg.
Cor. (C)
Tr. (C)
Timp.
Vl.
Vla.
Vc. e B.
ff
pp
1.
p

240
Fl.
Ob.
Cl.
Fg.
Cor. (C)
Vl.
Vla.
Vc. e B.
cresc.
zu 2
Tr. (C)
Timp.

250
zu 2
zu 2
zu 2
Fl.
Ob.
Cl.
Fg.
Cor. (C)
Tr. (C)
Timp.
Vl.
Vla.
Vc. e B.
ff
sf

Fl.
Ob.
Cl.
Fg.
Cor (C)
Tr. (C)
Timp.
Vl.
Vla.
Vc. e B.
fp
p
f
sf

260

zu 2

Fl.

Ob.

Cl.

Fg.

Cor (C)

Tr. (C)

Timp.

Vl.

Vla.

Vc. e B.

270
Fl.
Ob.
Cl.
Fg.
Cor. (C)
Tr. (C)
Timp.
Vl.
Vla.
Vc. e B.

280
Fl.
Ob.
Cl.
Fg.
zu 2
Cor. (C)
Tr. (C)
Timp.
Vl.
Vla.
Vc. u. Kb.
ff
sf

Fl.
Ob.
Cl.
Fg.
Cor. (C)
Tr. (C)
Timp.
Vl.
Vla.
Vc. e B.
zu 2
sf
ff

290
Fl.
Ob.
Cl.
Fg.
Cor. (C)
Tr. (C)
zu 2
zu 2
Timp.
Vl.
Vla.
Vc. e B.

II

Andante cantabile con moto (♪=120)
1. Flauto
2 Oboi
2 Clarinetti in C
2 Fagotti
2 Corni in F
2 Trombe in C
Timpani in C-G
I
Violino
II
pp
Viola
pp
Vc
Violoncello e Contrabasso
pp
10
Fl.
pp
Ob.
pp
Cl.
pp
zu 2
Fg.
pp
Cor. (F)
pp
Vl.
pp
Vla.
Vc.
B.
pp

20
Fl.
Ob.
Cl.
Fg.
Cor. (F)
Vl.
Vla.
Vc. e B.
Bassi
cresc.
sf
f
p
Vc.

30
Fl.
Ob.
Fg.
Cor. (F)
Vl.
Vla.
Vc.
zu 2
p
1.
Bassi
40
Cl.
cresc.
Vc. e B.
Vc.

Fl.
Ob.
Cl.
Fg.
Vl.
Vla.
Vc.
e B.
Bassi
50
zu 2
Cor.
(F)
Tr.
(C)
Timp.

Fl.
Ob.
Cl.
Fg.
Cor. (F)
Tr. (C)
Timp.
Vl.
Vla
Vc. e B.

60
Fl.
Ob.
Cl.
Fg.
Cor. (F)
Tr. (C)
Timp.
Vl.
Vla.
Vc. e B
p
70
1.
pp
cresc.
p cresc.
ff
p cresc.

Fl.
Ob.
Fg.
Cor. (F)
Vl.
Vla.
Vc. e B.
80
Fl.
Ob.
Cl.
Fg.
Cor F)
Timp
Vl.
Vla.
Vc. e B.

Fl.
Ob.
Cl
Fg.
Cor. (F)
Tr. (C)
Timp.
Vl.
Vla.
Vc. e B.
zu 2

90
Fl.
Ob.
zu 2
Cl.
Fg.
zu 2
Cor. (F)
cresc.
Tr. (C)
p
Timp.
tr
p
Vl.
p
Vla.
Vc. e B.
f

100
Ob.
Fg.
Vl.
Vc.
Vla.
Vc. e B.
cresc.
Bassi
Kb.
110
Fl.
Cl.
Cor. (F)
zu 2

120
Fl.
Ob.
Cl.
Fg.
Cor. (F)
Vl.
Vla.
Vc. e B.
cresc.
sf
f
p

130
Fl.
p
Vl.
p
Vla.
p
Vc.
e B.
p
Vc.
140
Fl.
1.
p
zu 2
Ob.
p
Cl.
p
zu 2
Fg.
p
Cor
(F)
p
Vl.
Vla.
Vc.
e B.
p
Bassi

Fl.
Cl.
Fg.
Cor. (F)
Vl.
Vla.
Vc. e B.
Vc.
150
Ob.
zu 2
Bassi

Fl.
Ob.
Cl
Fg.
Cor. (F)
Tr. (C)
Timp
Vl.
Vla.
Vc. e B
p
pp

160
Fl.
Ob.
Cl.
Fg.
Cor (F)
Tr. (C)
Timp.
Vl.
Vla.
Vc. e B.
170

Fl.
Ob.
Cl.
Fg.
Cor. (F)
Vl.
Vla.
Vc. e B.
180
Fl.
Ob.
Cl.
Fg.
Cor. (F)
Timp.
Vl.
Vla.
Vc. e B.
pizz.

Hb.
Cl.
Fg.
Cor. (F)
Vl
Vla.
Vc. e B.
190
Fl.
Ob.
Cl.
Fg.
Cor. (F)
Vl.
Vla.
Vc. e B.
arco

III

Menuetto Allegro molto e vivace (𝅗𝅥.=108)
2 Flauti
2 Oboi
2 Clarinetti in C
2 Fagotti
2 Corni in C
2 Trombe in C
Timpani in C.G
Violino I
Violino II
Viola
Violoncello e Contrabasso
zu 2
cresc.
10
Fl.
Ob.
Fg.
Vl.
Vla.
Vc.
B.

zu 2
20
Fl.
Ob.
Fg.
Vl.
Vla.
Vc.
B.
ff
sf
sfp
f
p
30
Fl.
Fg.
Vl.
Vla.
Vc.
B.
p
pp

1.
40
Ob.
pp
Fg.
Vl.
cresc.
Vla.
Vc.
e B.
Bassi
50
Fl.
f
ff
Cl.
Cor.
(C)
Tr.
(C)
Timp.

Fl.
zu 2
Ob.
Cl.
Fg.
zu 2
1.
Cor. (C)
Tr. (C)
Timp.
Vl.
Vla.
Vc. e B.

60
Fl.
Ob.
Cl.
Fg.
Cor. (C)
Tr. (C)
Timp.
Vl.
Vla.
Vc. e B.
1.
sf
p
zu 2
f

70
Fl.
cresc.
f
ff
sf
zu 2
Ob.
Cl.
cresc
Fg.
cresc.
Cor (C)
Tr. (C)
Timp.
Vl.
Vla.
Vc. e B.

Trio
80
Ob.
Cl.
Fg.
Cor
(C)
Vl.
p
90

100
Ob.
Cl.
Fg.
zu 2
Cor. (C)
Vl.
sf
110
Cl.
Cor. (C)
1. Vl.
p
decresc.
120
pp

Fl.
Ob.
Cl.
Fg.
Cor. (C)
Tr. (C)
Timp.
Vl.
Vla.
Vc. e B.

130
zu 2
Fl.
Ob.
Cl.
Fg.
Cor. (C)
Tr. (C)
Timp.
Vl.
Vla.
Vc. e B.
sf
Menuetto da Capo
(Pag. 50)

IV

Adagio (♪ = 63)
2 Flauti
2 Oboi
2 Clarinetti in C
2 Fagotti
2 Corni in C
2 Trombe in C
Timpani in C.G
Violino I
Violino II
Viola
Violoncello e Contrabasso
Allegro molto e vivace (𝅗𝅥 = 88)
10
Vl.
Vla.
Vc. e B.

Fg.
1.
p
Vl.
Vla.
Vc.
Bassi
Vc. e B.
p
20
Fl.
p
Ob.
p
Fg.
p
Cor. (C)
p
Vl.
cresc.
cresc.
Vla.
cresc.
Vc. e B.
cresc.

30
Fl.
Ob.
Cl.
Fg.
Cor. (C)
Tr. (C)
Timp.
Vl.
Vla.
Vc. e B.

Fl.
Ob.
Cl.
Fg.
Cor (C)
Tr. (C)
Timp
Vl.
Vla.
Vc. e B.
1.
40
f
sf
zu 2

Fl.
Ob.
Cl.
Fg.
Cor.
(C)
Tr.
(C)
Vl.
Vla.
Vc.
e B.
zu 2
50
sf
zu2
decresc.

60
Fl.
Ob.
Cl.
Fg.
Cor. (C)
Vl.
Vl.
Vc. e B.
1.
p
zu 2
cresc.
f
70
Vla.

zu 2

Fl.

Ob.

Fg.

zu 2

zu 2

Cor (C)

zu 2

Tr. (C)

Vl.

Vla.

Vc. e B.

80

Fl.

Ob.

Cl.

Fg.

zu 2

Cor. (C)

zu 2

Tr. (C)

Timp

Vl.

Vla.

Vc. e B.

90
Fl.
Ob.
Cl
Fg.
zu 2
Cor. (C)
zu 2
Tr. (C)
Timp.
Vl.
Vla.
Vc. e B.

1.
2.
Fl.
Ob.
Cl.
Fg.
Cor. (C)
Tr. (C)
Timp.
Vl.
Vla
Vc. e B.
1.
100
Ob.
Fg.
Vl.
Vla.
Vc. e B.
Vc.
Bassi

zu 2
110
Fl.
Ob.
Fg.
Vl.
Vla.
Vc.
e B.
ff
pp
120
p
fp
Vc.

Vl.
sempre p
sempre p
Vla.
sempre p
Vc. e B.
Vc.
sempre p
Fl.
130
1.
p
Ob.
1.
p
Fg.
p
Cor. (C)
zu 2
p
Vl.
Vla.
Vc.
Vc. e B.
Cb.
Bassi

Fl.
Ob.
Fg.
zu 2
cresc.
Cor. (C)
Vl.
Vla.
Vc. e B.
140
Cl.
Tr. (C)
Timp.
f
ff
sf

zu 2
150
Fl.
Ob.
Cl.
Fg.
Cor. (C)
Tr. (C).
Timp.
Vl.
Vla
Vc. e B.

160
Fl.
Ob.
Cl.
Fg.
Cor. (C)
Tr. (C)
Timp.
Vl.
Vla.
Vc. e B.
sf
ff

Fl.
Cl.
Fg.
Vl.
Vla.
Vc.
e B.
170
zu2
Cor
(C)
Vc.
Bassi

180
Fl.
Ob.
Cl.
Fg.
Cor. (C)
Tr. (C)
Vl.
Vla.
Vc. e B.
p
cresc.
f
zu 2
190
1.

200
Ob.
Cl.
1.
p
Fg.
Cor.
(C)
Vl.
Vla.
Vç.
e B.
1.
p cresc.
210
Fl.
Ob.
cresc.
f
Cl.
Fg.
cresc.
Cor.
(C)
cresc.
Vl.
cresc.
Vla.
Vc.
e B.

Fl.
Ob.
zu 2
Fg.
Cor. (C)
Vl.
Vla.
Vc. e B.
220
Fl.
Ob.
Cl.
Fg.
Cor. (C)
Tr. (C)
Timp.
Vl.
Vla.
Vc. e B.

E.E.3618

230
zu 2
Fl.
Ob.
Cl.
Fg.
Cor. (C)
Tr. (C)
Timp.
Vl.
Vla.
Vc. e B.
ff
sf

zu 2
1.
Fl.
Ob.
Cl.
Fg.
Cor. (C)
Tr. (C)
Timp
Vl.
Vla.
Vc. e B.

240
Fl.
Cl.
Fg.
Vl.
Vla.
Vc.
e B.
pp
p
f
Ob.
1.
250

260
Fl.
Cl.
zu 2
Fg.
Cor. (C)
Tr. (C)
Vl.
Vla.
Bassi
Vc. e B.
Fl.
Ob.
Cl.
Fg.
Cor. (C)
Tr. (C)
Timp.
Vl.
Vla.
Vc. e B.

270
Fl.
Ob.
Fg.
Cor. (C)
Vl.
Vla.
Vc. e B.
1.
280
Fl.
Ob.
Cl.
Fg.
Cor. (C)
Vl.
Vla.
Vc. e B.
cresc.

zu 2
290
Fl.
ff
sf
sf
zu 2
Ob.
ff
sf
sf
zu 2
Cl.
ff
sf
sf
Fg.
ff
sf
sf
Cor.
(C)
ff
sf
sf
Tr.
(C)
cresc.
ff
sf
sf
Timp.
p cresc.
ff
sf
sf
Vl.
ff
sf
sf
ff
sf
sf
Vla.
ff
sf
sf
Vc.
e B.
ff
sf
sf

300
zu 2
Fl.
ff
Ob.
ff
Cl.
ff
Fg.
ff
Cor.
(C)
ff
Tr.
(C)
zu 2
ff
Timp.
Vl.
ff
ff
Vla.
ff
Vc.
e B
ff